AFRICAN AMERICAN ANSWER BOOK

SPORTS

CHELSEA HOUSE PUBLISHERS

AFRICAN AMERICAN ANSWER BOOK

Available in Hardcover • 6 Titles

❏   Arts and Entertainment (0–7910–3201–9) $12.95

❏   Biography (0–7910–3203–5) $12.95

❏   Facts and Trivia (0–7910–3211–6) $12.95

❏   History (0–7910–3209–4) $12.95

❏   Science and Discovery (0–7910–3207–8) $12.95

❏   Sports (0–7910–3205–1) $12.95

Available in Paperback • 6 Titles

❏   Arts and Entertainment (0–7910–3202–7) $3.95

❏   Biography (0–7910–3204–3) $3.95

❏   Facts and Trivia (0–7910–3212–4) $3.95

❏   History (0–7910–3210–8) $3.95

❏   Science and Discovery (0–7910–3208–6) $3.95

❏   Sports (0–7910–3206–X) $3.95

Mail to: Chelsea House Publishers, Dept. Mail Order, P.O. Box 914, 1974 Sproul Road, Suite 400, Broomall, PA 19008-0914

Please send me the book(s) I have checked above.

My payment of $_____ is enclosed. (Please add $1.00 per order to cover postage and handling. PA residents add 6% sales tax.)

Method of payment: ❏ Cash   ❏ Check   ❏ Money Order

    ❏ Discover   ❏ VISA   ❏ MasterCard

Credit Card Number: _____

Expiration Date: _____

Phone Number: _____

Signature: _____

Please allow 6 weeks for delivery.

Name _____

Address _____

City _____ State _____ Zip _____

AFRICAN AMERICAN ANSWER BOOK

SPORTS

325 QUESTIONS
DRAWN FROM THE EXPERTISE OF
HARVARD'S DU BOIS INSTITUTE

R. S. Rennert

Chelsea House Publishers
New York   Philadelphia

CHELSEA HOUSE PUBLISHERS
EDITORIAL DIRECTOR Richard Rennert
EXECUTIVE MANAGING EDITOR Karyn Gullen Browne
COPY CHIEF Robin James
PICTURE EDITOR Adrian G. Allen
ART DIRECTOR Robert Mitchell
MANUFACTURING DIRECTOR Gerald Levine
ASSISTANT ART DIRECTOR Joan Ferrigno

AFRICAN AMERICAN ANSWER BOOK
SERIES ORIGINATOR AND ADVISER Ken Butkus
ASSISTANT EDITOR Annie McDonnell
DESIGNER John Infantino
PICTURE RESEARCHER Sandy Jones

Copyright © 1995 by Chelsea House Publishers, a
division of Main Line Book Co. All rights reserved.
Printed and bound in the United States of America.

3 5 7 9 8 6 4 2

ISBN 0-7910-3205-1
ISBN 0-7910-3206-X (pbk.)

PICTURE CREDITS
Library of Congress: p. 31; Negro Leagues Baseball
Museum, Inc.: p. 40; Owens Collection/Photo cour-
tesy Ohio State University: p. 34; Reuters/Bettmann: p.
18; UPI/Bettmann: pp. 10, 15, 23, 26, 46, 50.

CONTENTS

INTRODUCTION	6
QUESTIONS	7
ANSWERS	55
INDEX	62

INTRODUCTION

In creating the BLACK AMERICANS OF ACHIEVEMENT series for Chelsea House Publishers, I was fortunate enough to work closely with Nathan Irvin Huggins, one of America's leading scholars in the field of black studies and director of the W. E. B. Du Bois Institute for Afro-American Research at Harvard University. His innumerable contributions to the books have not only helped to make BLACK AMERICANS OF ACHIEVEMENT an award-winning series, but his expressed commitment to inform readers about the rich heritage and accomplishments of African Americans has encouraged Chelsea House to draw from his work and develop the 325 questions that make up this *African American Answer Book.*

Each of these briskly challenging questions has been designed to stimulate thought and discussion about African American history. The answers highlight either the leading figures of black America or focus on previously unsung yet equally inspiring African American heroes, their achievements, and their legacies.

You can use these questions to test your own knowledge or to stump your friends. Either way, you will find that this *African American Answer Book*—like its companion volumes—is bound to educate as well as entertain.

—R. S. R.

QUESTIONS

1. What professional baseball player finished his career with 755 home runs, which is the highest total in major league history?

    a - *Lou Brock*
    b - *Ernie Banks*
    c - *Henry Aaron*

2. What basketball superstar became the first African American to manage a major league sports team?

    a - *Oscar Robertson*
    b - *Lenny Wilkens*
    c - *Bill Russell*

3. What female track star set world records in the 100-meter and 200-meter dash?

    a - *Jackie Joyner-Kersee*
    b - *Althea Gibson*
    c - *Florence Griffith-Joyner*

4. Who are the only two brothers to ever hold the heavyweight boxing title?

    a - *Michael and Leon Spinks*
    b - *Jack and Joe Johnson*
    c - *George and Leonard Foreman*

5. Who became the first African American to win baseball's Most Valuable Player Award?

    a - *Jackie Robinson*
    b - *Willie Mays*
    c - *Hank Aaron*

6. George C. Poage was the first African American to win an Olympic medal in what two events?

    a - *200- and 400-meter hurdles*
    b - *Shot put and broad jump*
    c - *100- and 200-meter dash*

7. Jackie Robinson was the first African American to play major league baseball for what team?

    a - *Brooklyn Dodgers*
    b - *Milwaukee Braves*
    c - *New York Yankees*

8. Who was the first African American to lead the NFL in rushing?

    a - *Jim Brown*
    b - *Gale Sayers*
    c - *O. J. Simpson*

9. (True or False) John W. "Bud" Fowler was the first African American to play professional baseball.

10. When Don Newcombe played baseball for the Brooklyn Dodgers, what position did he play?

    a - *Outfielder*
    b - *Catcher*
    c - *Pitcher*

11. Who was known as "The Big O"?

    a - *Oscar Robertson*
    b - *Jesse Owens*
    c - *O. J. Simpson*

12. What heavyweight boxing champion defended his title against Muhammad Ali in 1971?

    a - *Mike Tyson*
    b - *Jack Johnson*
    c - *Joe Frazier*

13. Name the position that Gale Sayers played.

    a - *Linebacker*
    b - *Quarterback*
    c - *Running back*

14. Dehart Hubbard became the first African American to win the gold medal in what Olympic event?

    a - *High jump*
    b - *Broad jump*
    c - *Shot put*

15. (True or False) Willie Mays was the first African American to lead professional baseball in home runs.

16. What pitcher won 51 out of 55 games in the Negro leagues in 1905?

    a - *Andrew "Rube" Foster*
    b - *Satchel Paige*
    c - *Bob Gibson*

17. The University of North Carolina was the starting point for what NBA great?

    a - *Michael Jordan*
    b - *Wilt Chamberlain*
    c - *Magic Johnson*

18. How many times did Archie Griffin win the Heisman Trophy?

    a - *One*
    b - *Two*
    c - *Three*

19. What Hall of Fame pitcher once played basketball for the Harlem Globetrotters?

    a - *Bob Gibson*
    b - *Satchel Paige*
    c - *Ferguson Jenkins*

20. Who was the first African American quarterback to lead the NFL in passing?

    a - *James Harris*
    b - *Randall Cunningham*
    c - *Warren Moon*

21. Who was the first African American to win the Heisman Trophy?

    a - *Mike Garrett*
    b - *Archie Griffin*
    c - *Ernie Davis*

Baseball's all-time home run leader, Henry Aaron was also a Gold Glove Award–winning outfielder who compiled a lifetime .305 batting average and collected more extra-base hits and drove in more runs than any other player in major league history.

22. (True or False) Bill White was the first African American president of the National Football League.

23. In what year did the U.S. Postal Service issue a Jackie Robinson commemorative postage stamp?

    a - *1978*
    b - *1982*
    c - *1985*

24. What year marked the Harlem Globetrotters' first game?

    a - *1915*
    b - *1927*
    c - *1940*

25. (True or False) Charles Barkley was the first player in NBA history to win both the Most Valuable Player and Defensive Player of the Year awards in the same season.

26. Who was the first African American to start at quarterback in professional football?

    a - *Joe Gilliam*
    b - *Marlin Briscoe*
    c - *Doug Williams*

27. What African American lit the Olympic torch at the 1984 Summer Games?

    a - *Jesse Owens*
    b - *Rafer Johnson*
    c - *Willie Gault*

28. Which former major leaguer managed the Cleveland Indians in 1975?

    a - *Lou Brock*
    b - *Jackie Robinson*
    c - *Frank Robinson*

29. (True or False) Jim Brown was the first African American to play in the Rose Bowl.

30. What position did Doug Williams play in the 1988 Super Bowl?

    a - *Linebacker*
    b - *Running back*
    c - *Quarterback*

31. (True or False) Ken Griffey and Ken Griffey, Jr., were the only father and son to play at the same time on the same team.

32. (True or False) Magic Johnson is the only African American to have scored 100 points in a single NBA game.

33. In what year did Emmett Ashford become the first African American to umpire a major league baseball game?

    a - *1956*
    b - *1966*
    c - *1976*

34. Who was admitted into the Hall of Fame for being the best hitter in the Negro leagues?

    a - *Satchel Paige*
    b - *Andrew "Rube" Foster*
    c - *Josh Gibson*

35. Who was the first African American to join the Professional Golf Association?

    a - *Arthur Ashe*
    b - *Lee Elder*
    c - *Charles Sifford*

36. What was Satchel Paige's real name?

    a - *Louis*
    b - *Lester*
    c - *LeRoy*

37. (True or False) Hank Aaron never hit 50 home runs in one season.

38. What team played against Biddle College in the first African American college football game?

    a - *Tuskegee College*
    b - *Livingstone College*
    c - *Cheyney College*

39. Which of the following African Americans was once ranked as the number one tennis player in the world?

    a - *Bryan Shelton*
    b - *Arthur Ashe*
    c - *Chip Hooper*

40. Who was the first African American heavyweight boxing champion?

    a - *Muhammad Ali*
    b - *Jack Johnson*
    c - *Joe Louis*

41. Who was the first major league baseball player to steal more than 100 bases in a single season?

    a - *Lou Brock*
    b - *Willie Mays*
    c - *Maury Wills*

42. Who was the first black National League baseball player to hit 600 home runs?

    a - *Hank Aaron*
    b - *Willie Mays*
    c - *Ernie Banks*

43. What pitcher had the lowest earned run average (1.12 in 1968) in a single season?

    a - *Ferguson Jenkins*
    b - *Vida Blue*
    c - *Bob Gibson*

44. What major league baseball player hit three homers in a World Series game?

    a - *Rod Carew*
    b - *Reggie Jackson*
    c - *Willie Stargell*

45. Who was the first African American to play for the New York Yankees?

    a - *Ruben Amaro*
    b - *Elston Howard*
    c - *Reggie Jackson*

46. Hank Aaron began his career with what team?

    a - *Atlanta Braves*
    b - *Boston Braves*
    c - *Milwaukee Braves*

47. What team won the first Negro World Series?

    a - *Chicago Giants*
    b - *Detroit Stars*
    c - *Kansas City Monarchs*

48. Who was the first athlete to receive *Sports Illustrated's* Sportsman of the Year award after retiring from his professional career?

    a - *Arthur Ashe*
    b - *Willie Stargell*
    c - *O. J. Simpson*

49. What was Jackie Robinson's lifetime batting average?

    a - *.311*
    b - *.331*
    c - *.410*

50. Who was the first African American elected to the Baseball Hall of Fame?

    a - *Larry Doby*
    b - *Jackie Robinson*
    c - *Willie Mays*

51. Why did American sprinters Tommie Smith and John Carlos raise a fist during the medal ceremonies of the 1968 Olympics?

    a - *To show black power*
    b - *To show a symbol of black poverty in the U.S.*
    c - *To show a protest of the Vietnam War*

52. What former all-star first baseman became the highest-ranking black baseball executive in 1989 as president of the National League?

    a - *Jackie Robinson*
    b - *Hank Aaron*
    c - *Bill White*

53. What was Earl Monroe's nickname during his basketball career?

    a - *"Big M"*
    b - *"Magic"*
    c - *"The Pearl"*

54. Who holds the record for most free throws made in a single basketball game?

    a - *Michael Jordan*
    b - *Kareem Abdul-Jabbar*
    c - *Wilt Chamberlain*

55. What was Kareem Abdul-Jabbar's given name?

    a - *Lew Alcindor*
    b - *Andrew Foster*
    c - *Jim Brown*

56. Who did Floyd Patterson lose his title boxing fight to in 1962?

    a - *Muhammad Ali*
    b - *Rocky Marciano*
    c - *Sonny Liston*

57. Who led the NFL in rushing in eight of his nine seasons (for a total of 12,312 yards) and scored 126 touchdowns?

    a - *Walter Payton*
    b - *O. J. Simpson*
    c - *Jim Brown*

A colorful and often controversial personality in the world of sports, Muhammad Ali won a gold medal for boxing at the 1960 Olympics and captured the world heavyweight title three times.

58. (True or False) Andrew "Rube" Foster was the founding father of black baseball in the United States.

59. In 1962, Buck O'Neil became the first black coach of what baseball team?

    a - *New York Yankees*
    b - *Chicago Cubs*
    c - *Baltimore Orioles*

60. Which team was baseball's answer to the Harlem Globetrotters?

    a - *Chicago Pranksters*
    b - *St. Louis Funmakers*
    c - *Indianapolis Clowns*

61. What was boxing great Sugar Ray Robinson's real name?

    a - *Walker Smith, Jr.*
    b - *Henry Armstrong*
    c - *Archie Moore*

62. What NFL player, elected to the Hall of Fame, was the first African American to serve on the Minnesota Supreme Court?

　　a - *Alan Page*
　　b - *Jim Marshall*
　　c - *Joe Greene*

63. Wilt Chamberlain scored a record-setting 100 points in 1962 while playing for what team?

　　a - *New York Knicks*
　　b - *L.A. Lakers*
　　c - *Philadelphia Warriors*

64. Wilt Chamberlain set an NBA record for career rebounds with:

　　a - *18,250*
　　b - *21,226*
　　c - *23,924*

65. In 1971, Wilt Chamberlain set a league record for average points per game with:

　　a - *42.5*
　　b - *48.5*
　　c - *50.4*

66. Who became the first African American woman to win the prestigious Wimbledon singles title?

　　a - *Zina Garrison*
　　b - *Althea Gibson*
　　c - *Wilma Rudolph*

67. Who did Arthur Ashe beat in 1975 to become the first African American to win the singles title at Wimbledon?

　　a - *Bjorn Borg*
　　b - *Stan Smith*
　　c - *Jimmy Connors*

68. Jackie Robinson excelled in four sports at what university?

　　a - *University of South Carolina*
　　b - *University of California at Los Angeles*
　　c - *Notre Dame*

69. Jackie Joyner-Kersee won gold medals at the 1988 Olympic Games in Seoul, Korea, in what two events?

    a - *100- and 200-meter dash*
    b - *400- and 1600-meter relay*
    c - *Heptathlon and long jump*

70. Who became the first African American woman to sit on the International Olympic Committee?

    a - *Anita DeFrantz*
    b - *Lyle Stone*
    c - *Florence Griffith-Joyner*

71. Lyle Stone became the first black woman to play professional baseball in 1953 for the Indianapolis Clowns of the Negro American League. What position did she play?

    a - *First base*
    b - *Right field*
    c - *Second base*

72. In 1988, Debi Thomas won a medal in which Olympic event?

    a - *Speed skating*
    b - *Skiing*
    c - *Figure skating*

73. Lynette Woodard was the first woman to play for the:

    a - *Chicago White Sox*
    b - *Harlem Globetrotters*
    c - *U.S. Olympic Hockey Team*

74. (True or False) Charlie Sifford became the first USTA-approved tennis player in 1959.

75. (True or False) Tommie Smith and John Carlos gained international attention with a racial protest at the 1968 Olympics.

76. Boxing legend Joe Louis held the heavyweight crown for an unprecedented:

    a - *8 years*
    b - *9 years, 3 months*
    c - *11 years, 8 months*

A respected social activist and author, Arthur Ashe earned the distinction of being the first African American male professional tennis player to be ranked number one in the world.

77. What golfer became the first African American to play in the Masters?

    a - *Charlie Sifford*
    b - *Calvin Peete*
    c - *Lee Elder*

78. Who was the first African American to play in the National Hockey League?

    a - *Grant Fuhr*
    b - *Eldon Reddick*
    c - *Val James*

79. Who threw the pitch that made Henry Aaron baseball's home run king?

    a - *Al Downing*
    b - *Bob Gibson*
    c - *Jack Billingham*

80. On October 26, 1951, who knocked out Joe Louis in his last professional boxing fight?

    a - *Billy Conn*
    b - *Max Schmeling*
    c - *Rocky Marciano*

81. In 1961, who became the first black starting quarterback in the NFL?

    a - *Joe Gilliam*
    b - *Vince Evans*
    c - *Marlin Briscoe*

82. Marlin Briscoe was the starting quarterback for what football team?

    a - *Buffalo Bills*
    b - *Denver Broncos*
    c - *Oakland Raiders*

83. When Rickey Henderson stole his 939th base on May 1, 1991, whose record did he break?

    a - *Maury Wills*
    b - *Lou Brock*
    c - *Ty Cobb*

84. Jim Brown rushed for 12,312 yards during his nine-year career with what team?

    a - *Detroit Lions*
    b - *Pittsburgh Steelers*
    c - *Cleveland Browns*

85. What running back surpassed Jim Brown's rushing record of 12,312 yards?

    a - *O. J. Simpson*
    b - *Walter Payton*
    c - *Gale Sayers*

86. In what baseball park did Hank Aaron hit his 715th home run, breaking Babe Ruth's record?

    a - *Wrigley Field*
    b - *Atlanta-Fulton County Stadium*
    c - *Candlestick Park*

87. Muhammad Ali and Joe Frazier fought the first of their three fights in what city?

    a - *Atlantic City*
    b - *Manilla*
    c - *New York*

88. On March 8, 1971, Muhammad Ali lost a 15-round boxing match to Joe Frazier in what was called:

    a - *"Thrilla in Manilla"*
    b - *"World War III"*
    c - *"The Fight of the Century"*

89. During the March 1971 fight between Muhammad Ali and Joe Frazier, both fighters received record earnings of:

    a - *$1.5 million*
    b - *$2.5 million*
    c - *$3.5 million*

90. What famous baseball player who played for the Oakland A's and New York Yankees earned the nickname "Mr. October"?

    a - *Dave Winfield*
    b - *Reggie Jackson*
    c - *Elston Howard*

91. (True or False) Cito Gaston became the first African American baseball manager to win a World Series.

92. Willis Reed became the general manager of what professional basketball team?

    a - *Cleveland Cavaliers*
    b - *New Jersey Nets*
    c - *Denver Nuggets*

93. Hank Aaron became senior vice president and assistant to the president of what professional baseball team?

    a - *Milwaukee Brewers*
    b - *Atlanta Braves*
    c - *Houston Astros*

94. Eugene Upshaw, former defensive great with the Oakland Raiders, became executive director of the:

    a - *National Football League Manager's Association*
    b - *National Football League Player's Association*
    c - *National Football League*

95. What African American became executive director of the National Basketball Players Association?

    a - *Wes Unseld*
    b - *Willis Reed*
    c - *Charles Grantham*

96. How many gold medals did Jesse Owens win during the 1936 Summer Olympics?

    a - *4*
    b - *3*
    c - *2*

97. In 1923, Fritz Pollard became football's first black head coach of the:

    a - *Los Angeles Raiders*
    b - *Chicago Cardinals*
    c - *Hammond Pros*

98. Art Shell became football's second black coach of what team?

    a - *Detroit Lions*
    b - *Los Angeles Raiders*
    c - *Minnesota Vikings*

99. Who was named coach of the Minnesota Vikings in 1992?

    a - *Art Shell*
    b - *Dennis Green*
    c - *Bobby Mitchell*

100. Who became the first African American to own a significant interest in a major sports team, the Denver Nuggets?

    a - *Peter C. B. Bynoe*
    b - *Lenny Wilkens*
    c - *Wes Unseld*

101. In 1975, who became the first African American to manage a major league baseball team?

      a - *Cito Gaston*
      b - *Frank Robinson*
      c - *Hal McRae*

102. Who was nicknamed the "Buckeye Bullet"?

      a - *Ralph Metcalfe*
      b - *Bob Hayes*
      c - *Jesse Owens*

103. (True or False) Jesse Owens once set five world records in a single day.

104. Jackie Robinson began and ended his major league baseball career with what team?

      a - *New York Yankees*
      b - *Baltimore Orioles*
      c - *Brooklyn Dodgers*

105. Who broke Lou Brock's record of 938 stolen bases?

      a - *Rickey Henderson*
      b - *Bobby Bonds*
      c - *Vince Coleman*

106. Who became the first black player to quarterback a Super Bowl team to victory?

      a - *Randall Cunningham*
      b - *Doug Williams*
      c - *Vince Evans*

107. Doug Williams quarterbacked the Washington Redskins to a Super Bowl team to victory in what year?

      a - *1978*
      b - *1982*
      c - *1988*

108. Who was named MVP of the 1988 Super Bowl?

      a - *Ernest Byner*
      b - *Wilbur Marshall*
      c - *Doug Williams*

The greatest running back in National Football League history, Jim Brown set the all-time rushing record for a single game (237 yards), single season (1,863 yards), and career (12,312 yards).

109. Bill Russell became the first African American to coach a major league sports team in what year?

    a - *1967*
    b - *1970*
    c - *1977*

110. In what year did Jackie Robinson become the first African American to win the MVP Award in baseball?

    a - *1937*
    b - *1942*
    c - *1949*

111. Cornelius Johnson, Melvin Walker, and David Albritton excelled in what track-and-field event?

    a - *Shot put*
    b - *100-meter dash*
    c - *High jump*

112. Who was the first African American to win an Olympic medal in 200- and 400-meter hurdles?

    a - *Jesse Owens*
    b - *George C. Poage*
    c - *Carl Lewis*

113. Who was the first African American to play for the Brooklyn Dodgers?

> **a** - *Willie Mays*
> **b** - *Jackie Robinson*
> **c** - *Satchel Paige*

114. Who was the first African American woman to win an Olympic gold medal?

> **a** - *Alice Coachman*
> **b** - *Florence Griffith-Joyner*
> **c** - *Wilma Rudolph*

115. Sugar Ray Robinson won the 1951 World Middleweight Championship in a:

> **a** - *3rd round KO*
> **b** - *13th round KO*
> **c** - *10th round decision*

116. Whom did Sugar Ray Robinson beat in the 1951 middleweight championship?

> **a** - *Sonny Liston*
> **b** - *Jack Dempsey*
> **c** - *Jake Lamotta*

117. What National League pitcher was nicknamed "Dr. K"?

> **a** - *Dwight Gooden*
> **b** - *Anthony Young*
> **c** - *Don Newcombe*

118. In what World Series did Willie Mays's famous over-the-shoulder catch occur?

> **a** - *1954*
> **b** - *1955*
> **c** - *1956*

119. For what team was Willie Mays playing when his famous over-the-shoulder catch occurred?

> **a** - *Milwaukee Braves*
> **b** - *New York Giants*
> **c** - *San Francisco Giants*

120. (True or False) Henry Aaron is not only baseball's all-time home run leader but also its RBI leader.

121. Henry Aaron ended his career with how many home runs?

    a - *720*
    b - *735*
    c - *755*

122. Satchel Paige ended his major league career with how many victories?

    a - *28*
    b - *128*
    c - *228*

123. In what year did Walter Payton join the Chicago Bears?

    a - *1965*
    b - *1970*
    c - *1975*

124. In what year did Joe Frazier defend his title against Muhammad Ali?

    a - *1971*
    b - *1974*
    c - *1978*

125. In what year did Joe Frazier lose his title against George Foreman?

    a - *1968*
    b - *1970*
    c - *1973*

126. In what year did Dehart Hubbard become the first African American to win the Olympic gold medal in the broad jump?

    a - *1920*
    b - *1924*
    c - *1928*

127. Who was the first African American to lead professional baseball in home runs?

    a - *Larry Doby*
    b - *Willie Mays*
    c - *Andrew "Rube" Foster*

128. In what year did Rube Foster pitch and win 51 out of 55 games in the Negro leagues?

    a - *1905*
    b - *1915*
    c - *1935*

The first African American to break the racial barrier in both women's tennis and women's golf, Althea Gibson won both Wimbledon and the U.S. Nationals in 1957 and 1958.

129. Who was the first African American to play in the National Basketball Association?

    a - *Chuck Cooper*
    b - *Paul Robeson*
    c - *Marcus Haynes*

130. What African American sports legend was commemorated by a postage stamp in 1982?

    a - *Willie Mays*
    b - *Jackie Robinson*
    c - *Satchel Paige*

131. Who was the first player in NBA history to win both the MVP and Defensive Player of the Year awards in the same season?

    a - *Michael Jordan*
    b - *Charles Barkley*
    c - *Wilt Chamberlin*

132. Who was the first African American to play in the Rose Bowl?

    a - *Fritz Pollard*
    b - *Duke Slater*
    c - *Paul Robeson*

133. What was Bob Gibson's earned run average in 1968?

    a - *1.10*
    b - *1.12*
    c - *1.16*

134. O. J. Simpson gained how many yards during the 1973 football season?

    a - *1,500*
    b - *1,900*
    c - *2,003*

135. Who did Muhammad Ali knock out in 1974 to win the heavyweight title for the second time?

    a - *Joe Frazier*
    b - *Jimmy Ellis*
    c - *George Foreman*

136. What was O. J. Simpson's alma mater?

    a - *USC*
    b - *UCLA*
    c - *Notre Dame*

137. Carl Lewis won how many gold medals at the 1984 Summer Olympics?

    a - *4*
    b - *5*
    c - *6*

138. Henry Aaron finished his baseball career with what team?

    a - *Milwaukee Brewers*
    b - *Atlanta Braves*
    c - *Milwaukee Braves*

139. Who is acknowledged as the NFL's first outstanding black middle linebacker?

    a - *Sam Mills*
    b - *Mike Singletary*
    c - *Willie Lanier*

140. Paul Robeson, the famed singer and actor, was also a professional:

    a - *Football player*
    b - *Basketball player*
    c - *Baseball player*

141. In what year did Charles W. Follis become the first African American to play professional football?

   a - *1902*
   b - *1922*
   c - *1932*

142. In what year did the first African Americans, Chuck Cooper, Earl Lloyd, and Nathaniel Clifton, play in the NBA?

   a - *1935*
   b - *1948*
   c - *1950*

143. Charlie Taylor became the first African American to lead the NFL in receptions for two straight years while playing for what team?

   a - *San Francisco 49ers*
   b - *New York Giants*
   c - *Washington Redskins*

144. Carl Eller, Alan Page, and Jim Marshall were known in Minnesota as the:

   a - *Fearsome Threesome*
   b - *Steel Curtain*
   c - *Purple People Eaters*

145. Joe Greene, L. C. Greenwood, and Dwight White were known as the Pittsburgh Steelers':

   a - *Steel Curtain*
   b - *Iron City*
   c - *Iron and Steel*

146. Who played for the Los Angeles Rams and was a member of the "Fearsome Foursome"?

   a - *Joe Greene*
   b - *Rosey Grier*
   c - *Jim Marshall*

147. Who was the NFL's first African American coach?

   a - *Woody Strode*
   b - *Kenny Washington*
   c - *Emlen Tunnell*

148. (True or False) Willy T. Ribbs was the first African American to qualify and race in the Indianapolis 500.

149. Who played both major league baseball and football?

    a - *Bo Jackson*
    b - *Art Monk*
    c - *Willie Mays*

150. What famous African American boxer fought James Corbett in a 60-round draw?

    a - *George Godfrey*
    b - *Peter Jackson*
    c - *Jim Wharton*

151. In 1907, who did Jack Johnson defeat to win the heavyweight championship?

    a - *Jim Jeffries*
    b - *Jess Willard*
    c - *Tommy Burns*

152. What professional boxer was stripped of his title by the World Boxing Association after he was convicted of draft evasion?

    a - *Muhammad Ali*
    b - *Joe Frazier*
    c - *Sonny Liston*

153. How many times did Joe Louis defend his heavyweight boxing title?

    a - *15*
    b - *21*
    c - *26*

154. The Detroit sculpture of a powerful arm with a clenched fist is a memorial to what boxing great?

    a - *Jack Johnson*
    b - *Joe Louis*
    c - *Muhammad Ali*

155. What was Josh Gibson's nickname?

    a - *Grand Slammin' Josh*
    b - *The Babe Ruth of Negro Baseball*
    c - *Lightning Rod*

156. Who was regarded as the "Father of Modern Prize Fighting"?

    a - *Bill Richmond*
    b - *Andy Bowen*
    c - *George Dixon*

157. Why did Muhammed Ali throw his Olympic gold medal into the Ohio River?

    a - *To protest the Vietnam War*
    b - *To show disgust at America's racism*
    c - *To conform to his religious beliefs*

158. What was the name of the first African American baseball team?

    a - *St. Louis Stars*
    b - *Brooklyn Excelsiors*
    c - *Kansas City Monarchs*

159. What state was denied the opportunity to host the Super Bowl due to its failure to recognize Martin Luther King, Jr.'s birthday as a holiday?

    a - *Colorado*
    b - *Texas*
    c - *Arizona*

160. What Negro leagues team did Willie Mays play for?

    a - *Birmingham Black Barons*
    b - *Kansas City Monarchs*
    c - *Cuban Giants*

161. Whose professional baseball career was cut short by a paralyzing automobile accident?

    a - *Curt Flood*
    b - *Roy Campanella*
    c - *Elston Howard*

162. Who was the first African American to win a medal in Olympic competition?

    a - *Howard Drew*
    b - *George C. Poage*
    c - *Ralph Metcalfe*

The son of a former slave, Jack Johnson became the first African American to win the heavyweight boxing championship of the world.

163. What famous basketball player got 23,924 rebounds during his career?

    a - *Wilt Chamberlain*
    b - *Kareem Abdul-Jabbar*
    c - *Julius Erving*

164. What professional boxer was nicknamed the "Hit Man"?

    a - *Mike Tyson*
    b - *Joe Louis*
    c - *Thomas Hearns*

165. Who was the youngest boxer to win the heavyweight title?

    a - *Joe Frazier*
    b - *Muhammad Ali*
    c - *Mike Tyson*

166. (True or False) Michael and Leon Spinks were the only two brothers to hold the lightweight boxing title.

167. Who was the first heavyweight champion boxer to be trained by an African American?

    a - *Muhammad Ali*
    b - *Joe Louis*
    c - *Jack Johnson*

168. (True or False) Magic Johnson was the first basketball player to appear on a box of Wheaties.

169. (True or False) Gale Sayers was a member of the first all-black relay team to set a record in track and field.

170. (True or False) Bob Gibson and Reggie Jackson were the only two men to be World Series MVPs more than once.

171. What nickname was given to Henry Aaron for his lightning-quick home run swing?

    a - *Slammin' Hank*
    b - *Hammerin' Hank*
    c - *Hurricane Henry*

172. What famous football star danced with a Fort Worth ballet company?

    a - *Emmitt Smith*
    b - *Herschel Walker*
    c - *Walter Payton*

173. What famous athlete was a bodyguard for Robert F. Kennedy?

    a - *Rosey Grier*
    b - *Joe Greene*
    c - *David "Deacon" Jones*

174. Who was the first African American coach to win the NCAA National Basketball Championship?

    a - *John Cheyney*
    b - *John Thompson*
    c - *Bill Russell*

175. Who holds the record for most touchdowns scored from kickoff returns?

    a - *Jim Brown*
    b - *Timmy Brown*
    c - *Abner Haynes*

176. For what sport are Charles Wiltshire and Wendell Scott famous?

    a - *Auto racing*
    b - *Horse racing*
    c - *Golf*

177. What was Joe Louis's nickname?

    a - *The Greatest*
    b - *The Brown Bomber*
    c - *Joe Cool*

178. Who is the NFL's all-time career rushing leader?

    a - *O. J. Simpson*
    b - *Walter Payton*
    c - *Jim Brown*

179. (True or False) Lee Elder was the first African American golfer to tee off in the 1975 Masters Tournament.

180. In what year did Mike Tyson become the youngest heavyweight boxing champion in history?

    a - *1980*
    b - *1982*
    c - *1986*

181. Who did Muhammad Ali defeat on February 25, 1964, to win the heavyweight title?

    a - *Sonny Liston*
    b - *Floyd Patterson*
    c - *Joe Louis*

182. Who was the first African American professional pitcher?

    a - *Bob Gibson*
    b - *Dan Bankhead*
    c - *Don Newcombe*

183. Who is professional basketball's all-time career scoring leader?

    a - *Magic Johnson*
    b - *Wilt Chamberlain*
    c - *Kareem Abdul-Jabbar*

The first African American to win an Olympic gold medal, Jesse Owens dominated the track-and-field competition at the 1936 Olympics in Germany and shattered the Nazis' boast of white supremacy.

184. Who was the first African American professional football player?

    a - *Fritz Pollard*
    b - *Kenny Washington*
    c - *Marion Motley*

185. In what year did Althea Gibson become the first African American to win a major tennis title?

    a - *1957*
    b - *1960*
    c - *1965*

186. Who was the first African American to become a head coach for professional football?

    a - *Art Shell*
    b - *Dennis Green*
    c - *Bobby Mitchell*

187. In 1971, Cheryl White became the first African American female:

    a - *Golfer*
    b - *Jockey*
    c - *Tennis Player*

188. Who was the first African American pitcher in the American League?

    a - *Satchel Paige*
    b - *Vida Blue*
    c - *Don Newcombe*

189. Joe Louis Arena is located in what city?

    a - *Chicago*
    b - *Philadelphia*
    c - *Detroit*

190. What was the highest number of home runs Josh Gibson hit in a single season?

    a - *50*
    b - *70*
    c - *80*

191. On May 25, 1935, who set world records in three different track events?

    a - *Wilma Rudolph*
    b - *Jesse Owens*
    c - *Ralph Metcalfe*

192. Who won the 1968 Heisman Trophy?

    a - *Archie Griffin*
    b - *Mike Garrett*
    c - *O. J. Simpson*

193. (True or False) Debi Thomas was the first African American female athlete to win a medal in the winter Olympic Games.

194. Satchel Paige was elected to the Baseball Hall of Fame in what year?

    a - *1951*
    b - *1961*
    c - *1971*

195. What African American female athlete won three gold medals at the 1988 Seoul Olympics?

    a - *Florence Griffith-Joyner*
    b - *Wilma Rudolph*
    c - *Jackie Joyner-Kersee*

196. *Sugar Ray* is the title of a book about what boxing great?

    a - *Sugar Ray Leonard*
    b - *Sugar Ray Johnson*
    c - *Sugar Ray Robinson*

197. Who hit three home runs against the Los Angeles Dodgers, helping his team win the 1977 World Series?

    a - *Reggie Jackson*
    b - *Bobby Bonds*
    c - *Willie Stargell*

198. (True or False) Willie Stargell is the baseball star known for his famous over-the-shoulder catch.

199. Anita DeFrantz was only the second American:

    a - *Black umpire*
    b - *Recipient of the Bronze Medal of the Olympic Order*
    c - *Gold-medal swimmer*

200. Willie Mays ended his baseball career in 1973 with what team?

    a - *San Francisco Giants*
    b - *New York Mets*
    c - *New York Yankees*

201. What major league baseball team was the last to integrate their team?

    a - *New York Yankees*
    b - *Chicago Cubs*
    c - *Boston Red Sox*

202. Who was the first major league baseball player to steal 100 bases in a single season?

    a - *Lou Brock*
    b - *Willie Mays*
    c - *Maury Wills*

203. What African American started the popular custom of giving a teammate a "high five"?

  a - *Glenn Burke*
  b - *Ernie Banks*
  c - *Reggie Jackson*

204. What was Jackie Robinson's given name?

  a - *Jack Roberts*
  b - *Reginald Jackson*
  c - *Jack Roosevelt*

205. Who was the second African American to manage a major league baseball team?

  a - *Frank Robinson*
  b - *Larry Doby*
  c - *Cito Gaston*

206. Jackie Robinson appeared on what U.S. postage stamp?

  a - *5-cent*
  b - *7-cent*
  c - *15-cent*

207. (True or False) John Thompson was the first African American to coach a professional basketball team.

208. Who broke Jerry West's career playoff scoring record?

  a - *Kareem Abdul-Jabbar*
  b - *Wilt Chamberlain*
  c - *Earl Monroe*

209. When did Jackie Robinson break the color barrier by his entrance into baseball's National League?

  a - *1927*
  b - *1937*
  c - *1947*

210. What African American baseball player broke Ty Cobb's stolen bases record with 893?

  a - *Willie Mays*
  b - *Maury Wills*
  c - *Lou Brock*

211. Who was the National League's first African American pitcher?

> **a** - *Don Newcombe*
> **b** - *Bob Gibson*
> **c** - *Vida Blue*

212. Who was the National League's first African American Cy Young Award winner?

> **a** - *Bob Gibson*
> **b** - *Don Newcombe*
> **c** - *Ferguson Jenkins*

213. Elston Howard was the first African American to win what American League award?

> **a** - *Cy Young Award*
> **b** - *Most Valuable Player*
> **c** - *Batting Champion*

214. For what baseball team did Josh Gibson play?

> **a** - *St. Louis Cardinals*
> **b** - *Homestead Grays*
> **c** - *Kansas City Monarchs*

215. For what baseball team did Ernie Banks play?

> **a** - *Chicago White Sox*
> **b** - *Chicago Cubs*
> **c** - *Los Angeles Dodgers*

216. What were the Kansas City Monarchs?

> **a** - *All–African American football team*
> **b** - *All–African American basketball team*
> **c** - *All–African American baseball team*

217. Who was an eight-time batting champion?

> **a** - *Ernie Banks*
> **b** - *Rod Carew*
> **c** - *Lou Brock*

218. When was the professional Negro National League formed?

> **a** - *1898*
> **b** - *1920*
> **c** - *1925*

219. Who was the first African American pitcher to win the Cy Young Award in the American League?

    a - *Vida Blue*
    b - *Bob Gibson*
    c - *Don Newcombe*

220. Larry Doby played in what professional baseball league?

    a - *National*
    b - *American*
    c - *Continental*

221. Henry Aaron became the all-time home run king when he hit his 715th homer against what team?

    a - *Chicago Cubs*
    b - *Los Angeles Dodgers*
    c - *San Francisco Giants*

222. For what professional football team did Carl Weathers play?

    a - *Baltimore Colts*
    b - *Oakland Raiders*
    c - *Kansas City Chiefs*

223. What Chicago Bears football player was known as "The Refrigerator"?

    a - *Mike Singletary*
    b - *William Perry*
    c - *Walter Payton*

224. For what professional football team did Mercury Morris play?

    a - *Seattle Seahawks*
    b - *Buffalo Bills*
    c - *Miami Dolphins*

225. Jim Brown began his professional football career in 1957 with what team?

    a - *Pittsburgh Steelers*
    b - *Detroit Lions*
    c - *Cleveland Browns*

A Negro leagues star known for his blazing fastball, flawless control, and outrageous antics, Satchel Paige became at age 42 the major leagues' oldest rookie and the American League's first African American pitcher.

226. In 1950, the Cleveland Browns drafted Marion Motley to what position?

    a - *Linebacker*
    b - *Quarterback*
    c - *Fullback*

227. What football star became the first to rush for over 2,000 yards in a single season?

    a - *O. J. Simpson*
    b - *Jim Brown*
    c - *Walter Payton*

228. In the history of football, Johnny Greer was the first black:

    a - *Quarterback*
    b - *Head coach*
    c - *Referee*

229. What professional football player was known as the world's fastest human?

    a - *Willie Gault*
    b - *Jim Brown*
    c - *Bob Hayes*

230. Who was the first African American inductee into the Pro Football Hall of Fame?

    a - *Marion Motley*
    b - *Fletcher Joe Perry*
    c - *Emlen Tunnell*

231. Who became a major league rookie at the age of 42?

    a - *Jackie Robinson*
    b - *Satchel Paige*
    c - *Lou Brock*

232. Frank Robinson was the first African American manager of what major league baseball team?

    a - *Cleveland Indians*
    b - *Philadelphia Phillies*
    c - *Baltimore Orioles*

233. How tall is Kareem Abdul-Jabbar?

    a - *7 feet*
    b - *7 feet 2 inches*
    c - *7 feet 4 inches*

234. (True or False) Wilt Chamberlain is taller than Kareem Abdul-Jabbar.

235. John Thompson was the first African American basketball coach to win an NCAA Division Championship. What team did he coach to victory?

    a - *Syracuse*
    b - *Villanova*
    c - *Georgetown*

236. Earvin "Magic" Johnson played for what college basketball team?

    a - *University of Michigan*
    b - *UCLA*
    c - *Michigan State*

237. Who was known as Dr. J.?

    a - *Earvin Johnson*
    b - *Kareem Abdul-Jabbar*
    c - *Julius Erving*

238. Bill Russell won how many Most Valuable Player Awards?

    a - *1*
    b - *3*
    c - *5*

239. Louisiana's ban on boxing matches between blacks and whites was declared unconstitutional in:

    a - *1912*
    b - *1940*
    c - *1959*

240. For what professional sports team did "Meadowlark" Lemon play?

    a - *Harlem Globetrotters*
    b - *Renaissance Rens*
    c - *Chicago Romas*

241. The Harlem Globetrotters got their start in what city?

    a - *Harlem*
    b - *Philadelphia*
    c - *Chicago*

242. Before being christened the Harlem Globetrotters, what was this basketball team's name?

    a - *Savoy Big Five*
    b - *World Trotters*
    c - *Harlem Heat*

243. How many of the original five Harlem Globetrotters were from Harlem?

    a - *Five*
    b - *Three*
    c - *None*

244. For what team did Willie "Sweet Willie" Oliver, Al "Runt" Pullins, "Goose" Tatum, and Marcus Haynes play?

    a - *University of California at Los Angeles*
    b - *New York Knicks*
    c - *Harlem Globetrotters*

245. In 1960, who won the light-heavyweight Olympic gold medal?

    a - *Muhammad Ali*
    b - *Floyd Patterson*
    c - *Sonny Liston*

246. In 1957, Hank Aaron led what team to a World Series victory?

    a - *Atlanta Braves*
    b - *Milwaukee Brewers*
    c - *Milwaukee Braves*

247. Who coined Muhammad Ali's slogan, "Float like a butterfly, sting like a bee"?

    a - *Angelo Dundee*
    b - *Howard Cosell*
    c - *Drew "Bundini" Brown*

248. Walker Smith, Jr., is the real name of:

    a - *Herschel Walker*
    b - *Sugar Ray Robinson*
    c - *Emmitt Smith*

249. For what college team did Shaquille O'Neal play?

    a - *Louisiana State University*
    b - *Temple University*
    c - *University of Nevada at Las Vegas*

250. What football star led the NFL in rushing during the 1992–93 season and led his team to victory in Super Bowl XXVII?

    a - *Billy Simms*
    b - *Emmitt Smith*
    c - *Thurman Thomas*

251. Who was the first African American Olympic track-and-field participant?

    a - *Ralph Metcalfe*
    b - *Jesse Owens*
    c - *George Poage*

252. Who was one of the Harlem Wizards' greatest basketball attractions?

    a - *Bob Love*
    b - *Oscar Robertson*
    c - *George Bell*

253. Who knocked heavyweight boxer Muhammad Ali to the canvas in the 15th round of their first boxing match?

    a - *George Foreman*
    b - *Joe Frazier*
    c - *Leon Spinks*

254. Who was the first African American lightweight boxer to win the heavyweight title?

    a - *Henry Armstrong*
    b - *Archie Moore*
    c - *Michael Spinks*

255. Who held the heavyweight championship title from 1937 until his retirement in 1947?

    a - *Joe Louis*
    b - *Jack Johnson*
    c - *Floyd Patterson*

256. Sugar Ray Robinson ended his boxing career with a total of how many wins and knockouts?

    a - *105 Wins, 52 KO's*
    b - *152 Wins, 83 KO's*
    c - *174 Wins, 109 KO's*

257. Tiger Flowers was the first African American to win what boxing title?

    a - *Heavyweight*
    b - *Middleweight*
    c - *Lightweight*

258. Who was the first African American to compete in the U.S. Open tennis tournament?

    a - *Arthur Ashe*
    b - *John Shippen*
    c - *MaliVai Washington*

259. Who was the first African American teenager to win the Junior Girls singles title at Wimbledon?

    a - *Althea Gibson*
    b - *Zina Garrison*
    c - *Lori McNeil*

260. Who was the first African American to play on the Davis Cup tennis team?

    a - *Arthur Ashe*
    b - *John Shippen*
    c - *MaliVai Washington*

261. Who was the first African American to compete in the Olympics?

    a - *Jesse Owens*
    b - *George Poage*
    c - *Dehart Hubbard*

262. In 1968, Bob Beamon set an Olympic record in what event?

    a - *Long jump*
    b - *Broad jump*
    c - *High jump*

263. Congressman Ralph Metcalfe won a gold medal at what Olympics?

    a - *1936, Berlin*
    b - *1952, Helsinki*
    c - *1960, Rome*

264. (True or False) Calvin Peete was the first African American to play in the Masters golf tournament.

265. Chris Dickerson won what title in 1970?

    a - *Rushing*
    b - *Mr. America*
    c - *Golden Glove*

266. Herb Adderley was signed by what professional football team in 1961?

    a - *Chicago Bears*
    b - *Green Bay Packers*
    c - *Dallas Cowboys*

267. Who drilled an eleventh inning, game-winning home run in the sixth game of the 1991 World Series, defeating the Atlanta Braves?

    a - *Terry Pendleton*
    b - *Dave Winfield*
    c - *Kirby Puckett*

Crippled by polio at the age of four, Wilma Rudolph determinedly overcame her disability to amaze the world at the 1960 Rome Olympics, where she was known as "The Tennessee Tornado," the fastest woman on earth.

268. What nickname did Ozzie Smith earn due to his amazing acrobatics at shortstop?

    a - *The Octopus*
    b - *The Backstop*
    c - *The Wizard of Oz*

269. Who hit more home runs than anyone in the major leagues during the 1990 and 1991 seasons?

    a - *Paul Winfield*
    b - *Andre Dawson*
    c - *Cecil Fielder*

270. Who was named NBA Rookie of the Year in his first year as a center for the New York Knicks?

    a - *Cazzie Russell*
    b - *Bill Russell*
    c - *Willis Reed*

271. For what NBA team did Nate Thurmond play?

    a - *Chicago Bulls*
    b - *Philadelphia 76ers*
    c - *San Francisco Warriors*

272. Walt Bellamy played for what team in his first professional season?

    a - *Baltimore Bullets*
    b - *Chicago Packers*
    c - *Detroit Pistons*

273. What basketball player was named NBA Rookie of the Year while leading the Detroit Pistons to their first NBA championship playoff?

    a - *Oscar Robertson*
    b - *Dave Bing*
    c - *Earl Monroe*

274. What is basketball star Michael Jordan's nickname?

    a - *Jet Jordan*
    b - *Dr. J.*
    c - *Air Jordan*

275. What basketball star is referred to as "The Mailman"?

    a - *Charles Barkley*
    b - *Moses Malone*
    c - *Karl Malone*

276. What basketball star center perfected a new shot called the "skyhook"?

    a - *Wilt Chamberlain*
    b - *Bill Russell*
    c - *Kareem Abdul-Jabbar*

277. In the NBA inaugural year, 1949–50, how many African American basketball players were in the league?

    a - *0*
    b - *5*
    c - *16*

278. Chuck Cooper was the first African American to play NBA basketball. With what team did he make his debut?

    a - *Philadelphia 76ers*
    b - *New York Knicks*
    c - *Boston Celtics*

279. What basketball star perfected the "turn-around jumper"?

    a - *Walt Frazier*
    b - *Bobby Dandridge*
    c - *Elvin Hayes*

280. Who became the first African American running back to rush more than 1,000 yards in a single season?

    a - *Marion Motley*
    b - *Joe Perry*
    c - *Buddy Young*

281. What football great made several advertising and commercial endorsements, paving the way in an area of sports that was previously off-limits to black sports stars?

    a - *Jim Brown*
    b - *Gale Sayers*
    c - *O. J. Simpson*

282. Which of the following football stars was not a middle linebacker?

    a - *Willie Lanier*
    b - *Mike Singletary*
    c - *David "Deacon" Jones*

283. During the 1970s, what boxing great defeated Thomas Hearns, Wilfredo Benitez, and Roberto Duran?

    a - *Sugar Ray Robinson*
    b - *Sugar Ray Leonard*
    c - *Muhammad Ali*

284. What sports team was referred to by many as the "Dream Team"?

    a - *Chicago Bulls*
    b - *Pittsburgh Steelers*
    c - *1992 Olympic basketball team*

285. At the 1992 Summer Olympics, in what event did Jackie Joyner-Kersee win a gold medal?

    a - *Long jump*
    b - *Heptathlon*
    c - *High jump*

286. In 1988, what basketball player became the first NBA player to reach 37,000 career points?

    a - *Magic Johnson*
    b - *Julius Erving*
    c - *Kareem Abdul-Jabbar*

287. What professional basketball star returned to the NBA after successfully combating drug addiction and commented, "People say you almost lost basketball. Well, I almost lost my life."?

    a - *Nate Archibald*
    b - *John Lucas*
    c - *Bill Russell*

288. While playing football for Notre Dame, what nickname did Raghib Ismail earn?

    a - *Bullet*
    b - *Torpedo*
    c - *Rocket*

289. Which of the following football players is a member of the Washington Redskins' "Posse"?

    a - *Charlie Taylor*
    b - *Art Monk*
    c - *Wilbur Marshall*

290. Abdul-Jabbar, Johnson, Worthy, and Wilkes led the Los Angeles Lakers to how many NBA titles?

    a - *2*
    b - *4*
    c - *6*

291. Luis Aparicio earned a Gold Glove at what position?

    a - *Shortstop*
    b - *Third baseman*
    c - *First baseman*

292. Olympic star Bob Hayes played what position for the Dallas Cowboys?

    a - *Running back*
    b - *Cornerback*
    c - *Wide receiver*

The winningest player in National Basketball Association (NBA) history, Bill Russell was voted the NBA's Most Valuable Player (MVP) five times and later became the first African American to coach an NBA team.

293. What professional sport did Charlie Sifford play?

    a - *Golf*
    b - *Tennis*
    c - *Basketball*

294. What professional sport did Lee Elder play?

    a - *Tennis*
    b - *Football*
    c - *Golf*

295. In what event did Major Taylor become "the world's fastest"?

    a - *Auto racing*
    b - *Sprinting*
    c - *Bicycle racing*

296. Who was a pioneer in developing the interest of women in athletics?

    a - *Alice Coachman*
    b - *Anita Grant*
    c - *Lula Hymes*

297. What do Mike Garrett, Ernie Davis, and Billy Simms have in common?

    a - *All played football at the University of Oklahoma*
    b - *All won the Heisman Trophy*
    c - *All played football for the Detroit Lions*

298. Bobby Bell played what position for the Kansas City Chiefs?

    a - *Cornerback*
    b - *Linebacker*
    c - *Fullback*

299. Lenny Moore and Liddell Mitchell played for what football team?

    a - *Miami Dolphins*
    b - *Greenbay Packers*
    c - *Baltimore Colts*

300. (True or False) Emmett Ashford was the first black umpire in organized baseball.

301. For what professional football team did David "Deacon" Jones play?

    a - *San Francisco 49ers*
    b - *Los Angeles Rams*
    c - *Dallas Cowboys*

302. For what team did Ed "Too Tall" Jones play football?

    a - *Dallas Cowboys*
    b - *Chicago Bears*
    c - *New York Giants*

303. In 1960, what African American football star became the AFL's first "Player of the Year"?

    a - *Abner Haynes*
    b - *Paul Lowe*
    c - *Mike Garrett*

304. In 1960, Abner Haynes played for what AFL team?

    a - *San Diego Chargers*
    b - *Kansas City Chiefs*
    c - *Dallas Texans*

305. Otis Taylor was a standout player for what football team in the late 1960s?

    a - *Buffalo Bills*
    b - *Houston Oilers*
    c - *Kansas City Chiefs*

306. In what professional sports did Gene "Big Daddy" Lipscomb earn stardom?

    a - *Basketball and boxing*
    b - *Football and boxing*
    c - *Football and wrestling*

307. Willie Mays received a bonus of how much money when he signed with the New York Giants?

    a - *$5,000*
    b - *$10,000*
    c - *$25,000*

308. With what professional baseball team did Ernie Banks start and end his career?

    a - *St. Louis Cardinals*
    b - *Chicago Cubs*
    c - *Philadelphia Phillies*

309. Who was the first baseball player to win the honor of "Most Valuable Player" in both the National and American baseball leagues?

    a - *Hank Aaron*
    b - *Dave Winfield*
    c - *Frank Robinson*

310. What baseball team did Frank Robinson help win the pennant in 1961?

    a - *Cincinnati Reds*
    b - *Baltimore Orioles*
    c - *Cleveland Indians*

311. What baseball team did Frank Robinson help win the World Series in 1966?

    a - *Baltimore Orioles*
    b - *Cincinnati Reds*
    c - *Cleveland Indians*

312. Bill Russell was the first African American basketball coach of what team?

    a - *New York Knicks*
    b - *Washington Bullets*
    c - *Boston Celtics*

313. Julius Erving began his professional basketball career with what team?

    a - *Philadelphia 76ers*
    b - *Virginia Squires*
    c - *Houston Mavericks*

314. Basketball star Willis Reed became the coach of what team in 1977?

    a - *Boston Celtics*
    b - *Washington Capitals*
    c - *New York Knicks*

315. What do Jimmy Winkfield and Isaac Murphy have in common?

    a - *Entered professional auto racing same year*
    b - *Both won the Heisman Trophy*
    c - *Both won the Kentucky Derby twice in succession*

316. Who was the first African American to lead an NFL officiating crew?

    a - *Gil Marchman*
    b - *Len Williams*
    c - *Johnny Grier*

317. What African American became a league supervisor, the highest ranking sports official?

    a - *Leo Miles*
    b - *Hue Hollins*
    c - *Johnny Grier*

318. Eric Gregg, Charlie Williams, and Charlie Merriweather are:

    a - *NFL referees*
    b - *Major league baseball umpires*
    c - *NBA officials*

319. What professional boxer knocked out Carl the "Truth" Williams in the first minute and a half of the first round, the fifth fastest title bout in boxing history?

    a - *Joe Frazier*
    b - *Muhammad Ali*
    c - *Mike Tyson*

320. Who played in the 1971 and 1979 World Series and was named Most Valuable Player of the 1979 series?

    a - *Frank Robinson*
    b - *Willie Stargell*
    c - *Reggie Jackson*

321. What track star won four gold medals at the 1984 Summer Olympics?

    a - *Carl Lewis*
    b - *Edwin Moses*
    c - *Rafer Johnson*

322. What baseball player was nicknamed the "Say-Hey Kid"?

    a - *Lou Brock*
    b - *Jackie Robinson*
    c - *Willie Mays*

323. What influential baseball figure hired Jackie Robinson?

    a - *Judge Kenesaw Mountain Landis*
    b - *Babe Ruth*
    c - *Branch Rickey*

324. Milt Campbell became the first African American to win the decathlon during what Olympic Games?

    a - *1936*
    b - *1944*
    c - *1952*

325. Arthur Ashe retired from professional tennis due to what?

    a - *Leg injuries*
    b - *Heart problems*
    c - *Severe arthritis*

ANSWERS

1. c **Henry Aaron**
2. c **Bill Russell**
3. c **Florence Griffith-Joyner**
4. a **Michael and Leon Spinks**
5. a **Jackie Robinson**
6. a **200-and 400-meter hurdles**
7. a **Brooklyn Dodgers**
8. a **Jim Brown**
9. **True**
10. c **Pitcher**
11. a **Oscar Robertson**
12. c **Joe Frazier**
13. c **Running back**
14. b **Broad jump**
15. **False - Larry Doby**
16. a **Andrew "Rube" Foster**
17. a **Michael Jordan**
18. b **Two**
19. a **Bob Gibson**
20. a **James Harris**
21. c **Ernie Davis**
22. **False - National Baseball League**
23. b **1982**
24. b **1927**
25. **False - Michael Jordan**
26. b **Marlin Briscoe**
27. b **Rafer Johnson**
28. c **Frank Robinson**
29. **False - Fritz Pollard**
30. c **Quarterback**
31. **True**
32. **False - Wilt Chamberlain**
33. b **1966**
34. c **Josh Gibson**
35. c **Charles Sifford**
36. b **LeRoy**
37. **True**

38. b Livingstone College
39. b Arthur Ashe
40. b Jack Johnson
41. c Maury Wills
42. b Willie Mays
43. c Bob Gibson
44. b Reggie Jackson
45. b Elston Howard
46. c Milwaukee Braves
47. c Kansas City Monarchs
48. a Arthur Ashe
49. a .311
50. b Jackie Robinson
51. a To show black power
52. c Bill White
53. c "The Pearl"
54. c Wilt Chamberlain
55. a Lew Alcindor
56. c Sonny Liston
57. c Jim Brown
58.   True
59. b Chicago Cubs
60. c Indianapolis Clowns
61. a Walker Smith
62. a Alan Page
63. c Philadelphia Warriors
64. c 23,924
65. c 50.4
66. b Althea Gibson
67. c Jimmy Connors
68. b University of California at Los Angeles
69. c Heptathlon and long jump
70. a Anita DeFrantz
71. c Second base
72. c Figure skating
73. b Harlem Globetrotters
74.   False - PGA-approved golfer
75.   True
76. c 11 years, 8 months
77. c Lee Elder
78. c Val James
79. a Al Downing
80. c Rocky Marciano
81. c Marlin Briscoe
82. b Denver Broncos
83. b Lou Brock
84. c Cleveland Browns
85. b Walter Payton
86. b Atlanta–Fulton County Stadium

87. c New York
88. c "The Fight of the Century"
89. b $2.5 million
90. b Reggie Jackson
91. True
92. b New Jersey Nets
93. b Atlanta Braves
94. b National Football League Player's Association
95. c Charles Grantham
96. a 4
97. c Hammond Pros
98. b Los Angeles Raiders
99. b Dennis Green
100. a Peter C. B. Bynoe
101. b Frank Robinson
102. c Jesse Owens
103. True
104. c Brooklyn Dodgers
105. a Rickey Henderson
106. b Doug Williams
107. c 1988
108. c Doug Williams
109. a 1967
110. c 1949
111. c High jump
112. b George C. Poage
113. b Jackie Robinson
114. a Alice Coachman
115. b 13th-round KO
116. c Jake Lamotta
117. a Dwight Gooden
118. a 1954
119. b New York Giants
120. b True
121. c 755
122. a 28
123. b 1975
124. a 1971
125. c 1973
126. b 1924
127. b Larry Doby
128. a 1905
129. a Chuck Cooper
130. b Jackie Robinson
131. a Michael Jordan
132. a Fritz Pollard
133. b 1.12
134. c 2,003
135. c George Foreman

136. a USC
137. a 4
138. b Atlanta Braves
139. c Willie Lanier
140. a Football player
141. a 1902
142. c 1950
143. c Washington Redskins
144. c Purple People Eaters
145. a Steel Curtain
146. b Rosey Grier
147. c Emlen Tunnell
148. True
149. a Bo Jackson
150. b Peter Jackson
151. c Tommy Burns
152. a Muhammad Ali
153. c 26
154. b Joe Louis
155. b The Babe Ruth of Negro Baseball
156. a Bill Richmond
157. b To show disgust at America's racism
158. b Brooklyn Excelsiors
159. c Arizona
160. a Birmingham Black Barons
161. b Roy Campanella
162. b George C. Poage
163. a Wilt Chamberlain
164. c Thomas Hearns
165. c Mike Tyson
166. False - Heavyweight
167. b Joe Louis
168. False - Michael Jordan
169. False - O. J. Simpson
170. True
171. b Hammerin' Hank
172. b Herschel Walker
173. a Rosey Grier
174. b John Thompson
175. b Timmy Brown
176. a Auto racing
177. b The Brown Bomber
178. b Walter Payton
179. True
180. c 1986
181. a Sonny Liston
182. b Dan Bankhead
183. c Kareem Abdul-Jabbar
184. a Fritz Pollard

185. a **1957**
186. a **Art Shell**
187. b **Jockey**
188. a **Satchel Paige**
189. c **Detroit**
190. c **80**
191. b **Jesse Owens**
192. c **O. J. Simpson**
193.   **True**
194. c **1971**
195. a **Florence Griffith-Joyner**
196. c **Sugar Ray Robinson**
197. a **Reggie Jackson**
198.   **False -Willie Mays**
199. b **Recipient of the Bronze Medal of the Olympic Order**
200. b **New York Mets**
201. c **Boston Red Sox**
202. c **Maury Wills**
203. a **Glenn Burke**
204. c **Jack Roosevelt**
205. b **Larry Doby**
206. c **15-cent**
207.   **False -Bill Russell**
208. a **Kareem Abdul-Jabbar**
209. c **1947**
210. c **Lou Brock**
211. a **Don Newcombe**
212. b **Don Newcombe**
213. b **Most Valuable Player**
214. b **Homestead Grays**
215. b **Chicago Cubs**
216. c **All–African American baseball team**
217. b **Rod Carew**
218. b **1920**
219. a **Vida Blue**
220. b **American**
221. b **Los Angeles Dodgers**
222. b **Oakland Raiders**
223. b **William Perry**
224. c **Miami Dolphins**
225. c **Cleveland Browns**
226. c **Fullback**
227. a **O. J. Simpson**
228. c **Referee**
229. c **Bob Hayes**
230. c **Emlen Tunnell**
231. b **Satchel Paige**
232. a **Cleveland Indians**

233. b **7 feet 2 inches**
234.   **False**
235. c **Georgetown**
236. c **Michigan State**
237. c **Julius Erving**
238. c **5**
239. c **1959**
240. a **Harlem Globetrotters**
241. c **Chicago**
242. a **Savoy Big Five**
243. c **None**
244. c **Harlem Globetrotters**
245. a **Muhammad Ali**
246. c **Milwaukee Braves**
247. c **Drew "Bundini" Brown**
248. b **Sugar Ray Robinson**
249. a **Louisiana State University**
250. b **Emmitt Smith**
251. c **George Poage**
252. c **George Bell**
253. b **Joe Frazier**
254. c **Michael Spinks**
255. a **Joe Louis**
256. c **174 Wins, 109 KO's**
257. b **Middleweight**
258. b **John Shippen**
259. b **Zina Garrison**
260. a **Arthur Ashe**
261. b **George Poage**
262. a **Long jump**
263. a **1936, Berlin**
264.   **False - Lee Elder**
265. b **Mr. America**
266. b **Green Bay Packers**
267. c **Kirby Puckett**
268. c **The Wizard of Oz**
269. c **Cecil Fielder**
270. c **Willis Reed**
271. c **San Francisco Warriors**
272. b **Chicago Packers**
273. b **Dave Bing**
274. c **Air Jordan**
275. c **Karl Malone**
276. c **Kareem Abdul-Jabbar**
277. a **0**
278. c **Boston Celtics**
279. c **Elvin Hayes**
280. b **Joe Perry**
281. c **O. J. Simpson**

282. c David "Deacon" Jones
283. b Sugar Ray Leonard
284. c 1992 Olympic basketball team
285. b Heptathlon
286. c Kareem Abdul-Jabbar
287. b John Lucas
288. c Rocket
289. b Art Monk
290. b 4
291. a Shortstop
292. c Wide receiver
293. a Golf
294. c Golf
295. c Bicycle racing
296. b Anita Grant
297. b All won the Heisman Trophy
298. b Linebacker
299. c Baltimore Colts
300.   True
301. b Los Angeles Rams
302. a Dallas Cowboys
303. a Abner Haynes
304. c Dallas Texans
305. c Kansas City Chiefs
306. c Football and wrestling
307. a $5,000
308. b Chicago Cubs
309. c Frank Robinson
310. a Cincinnati Reds
311. a Baltimore Orioles
312. c Boston Celtics
313. b Virginia Squires
314. c New York Knicks
315. c Both won the Kentucky Derby twice
        in succession
316. c Johnny Grier
317. a Leo Miles
318. b Major league baseball umpires
319. c Mike Tyson
320. b Willie Stargell
321. a Carl Lewis
322. c Willie Mays
323. c Branch Rickey
324. a 1936
325. b Heart problems

INDEX

Aaron, Henry, 7, 12, 13, 14, 18, 19, 20, 24, 25, 27, 39, 43, 52
Abdul-Jabbar, Kareem, 14, 31, 32, 33, 37, 41, 47, 49
Adderley, Herb, 45
Albritton, David, 23
Alcindor, Lew. See Abdul-Jabbar, Kareem
Ali, Muhammad, 8, 12, 15, 20, 27, 29, 30, 31, 32, 33, 43, 48, 53
Amaro, Ruben, 13
Aparicio, Luis, 49
Archibald, Nate, 49
Armstrong, Henry, 15, 44
Ashe, Arthur, 12, 13, 16, 44, 54
Ashford, Emmett, 11, 51

Bankhead, Dan, 33
Banks, Ernie, 7, 12, 37, 38, 52
Barkley, Charles, 10, 26, 47
Beamon, Bob, 45
Bell, Bobby, 51
Bell, George, 43
Bellamy, Walt, 47
Benitez, Wilfredo, 48
Billingham, Jack, 18
Bing, Dave, 47
Blue, Vida, 13, 35, 38, 39
Bonds, Bobby, 22, 36
Bowen, Andy, 30
Briscoe, Marlin, 11, 19
Brock, Lou, 7, 11, 12, 19, 22, 36, 37, 38, 41, 54
Brown, Drew "Bundini," 43
Brown, Jim, 8, 11, 14, 19, 32, 33, 39, 40, 48
Brown, Timmy, 32
Burke, Glenn, 37
Burns, Tommy, 29
Byner, Ernest, 22
Bynoe, Peter C. B., 21

Campanella, Roy, 30
Campbell, Milt, 54
Carew, Rod, 13, 38
Carlos, John, 14, 17
Chamberlain, Wilt, 9, 14, 16, 26, 31, 33, 37, 41, 47
Cheyney, John, 32
Clifton, Nathaniel, 28
Coachman, Alice, 24, 50
Cobb, Ty, 19, 37
Coleman, Vince, 22
Conn, Billie, 19
Connors, Jimmy, 16
Cooper, Chuck, 26, 28, 47
Corbett, James, 29
Cosell, Howard, 43
Cunningham, Randall, 9, 22

Dandridge, Bobby, 48
Davis, Ernie, 9, 50
Dawson, Andre, 46
DeFrantz, Anita, 17, 36
Dempsey, Jack, 24
Dickerson, Chris, 45
Dixon, George, 30
Doby, Larry, 13, 25, 37, 39
Downing, Al, 18
Drew, Howard, 30
Dundee, Angelo, 43
Duran, Roberto, 48

Elder, Lee, 12, 18, 33, 50
Eller, Carl, 28
Ellis, Jimmy, 27
Erving, Julius, 31, 41, 49, 53
Evans, Vince, 19, 22

Fielder, Cecil, 46
Flood, Curt, 30
Flowers, Tiger, 44
Follis, Charles W., 28
Foreman, George, 7, 25, 27, 44
Foreman, Leonard, 7
Foster, Andrew "Rube," 9, 11, 14, 25
Fowler, John W. "Bud," 8
Frazier, Joe, 8, 20, 25, 27, 29, 31, 44, 53
Frazier, Walt, 48
Fuhr, Grant, 18

Garrett, Mike, 9, 35, 50, 51
Garrison, Zina, 16, 44
Gaston, Cito, 20, 22, 37
Gault, Willie, 11, 40
Gibson, Althea, 7, 16, 34, 44
Gibson, Bob, 9, 13, 18, 27, 32, 33, 38, 39
Gibson, Josh, 11, 29, 35, 38
Gilliam, Joe, 11, 19
Godfrey, George, 29
Gooden, Dwight, 24
Grant, Anita, 50
Grantham, Charles, 21
Green, Dennis, 21, 34
Greene, Joe, 16, 28, 32
Greenwood, L. C., 28
Greer, Johnny, 40
Gregg, Eric, 53
Grier, Johnny, 53
Grier, Rosey, 28, 32
Griffey, Ken, 11
Griffey, Ken, Jr., 11
Griffin, Archie, 9, 35
Griffith-Joyner, Florence, 7, 17, 24, 36

Harris, James, 9
Hayes, Bob, 22, 40, 49
Hayes, Elvin, 48

62

Haynes, Abner, 32, 51
Haynes, Marcus, 26, 42
Hearns, Thomas, 31, 48
Henderson, Rickey, 19, 23
Hollins, Hue, 53
Hooper, Chip, 12
Howard, Elston, 13, 20, 30, 38
Hubbard, Dehart, 9, 25, 45
Hymes, Lula, 50

Ismail, Raghib, 49

Jackson, Bo, 29
Jackson, Peter, 29
Jackson, Reggie, 13, 20, 32, 36, 37, 54
James, Val, 18
Jeffries, Jim, 29
Jenkins, Ferguson, 9, 13, 38
Johnson, Cornelius, 23
Johnson, Earvin "Magic," 9, 11, 32,
   33, 41, 49
Johnson, Jack, 7, 8, 12, 29, 32, 44
Johnson, Joe, 7
Johnson, Rafer, 11, 54
Johnson, Sugar Ray, 36
Jones, David "Deacon," 32, 48, 51
Jones, Ed "Too Tall," 51
Jordan, Michael, 9, 14, 26, 47
Joyner-Kersee, Jackie, 7, 17, 36, 48

LaMotta, Jake, 24
Landis, Judge Kenesaw Mountain, 54
Lanier, Willie, 27, 48
Lemon, "Meadowlark," 42
Leonard, Sugar Ray, 36, 48
Lewis, Carl, 23, 27, 54
Lipscomb, Gene "Big Daddy," 52
Liston, Sonny, 15, 24, 29, 33, 43
Lloyd, Earl, 28
Louis, Joe, 12, 17, 19, 29, 31, 32, 33,
   35, 44
Lowe, Paul, 51
Lucas, John, 49

McNeil, Lori, 44
McRae, Hal, 22
Malone, Karl, 47
Malone, Moses, 47
Marchman, Gil, 53
Marciano, Rocky, 15, 19
Marshall, Jim, 16, 28
Marshall, Wilbur, 22, 49
Mays, Willie, 7, 9, 12, 13, 24, 25, 26,
   29, 30, 36, 37, 52, 54
Merriweather, Charlie, 53
Metcalfe, Ralph, 22, 30, 35, 43, 45
Miles, Leo, 53
Mills, Sam, 27
Mitchell, Bobby, 21, 34
Mitchell, Liddell, 51

Monk, Art, 29, 49
Monroe, Earl, 14, 37, 47
Moon, Warren, 9
Moore, Archie, 15, 44
Moore, Lenny, 51
Morris, Mercury, 39
Moses, Edwin, 54
Motley, Marion, 34, 40, 41, 48
Murphy, Isaac, 53

Newcombe, Don, 8, 24, 33, 35, 38, 39

Oliver, Willie "Sweet Willie," 42
O'Neal, Shaquille, 43
O'Neil, Buck, 15
Owens, Jesse, 8, 11, 21, 22, 23, 35,
   43, 45

Page, Alan, 16, 28
Paige, Satchel, 9, 11, 12, 24, 25, 26,
   35, 41
Patterson, Floyd, 14, 33, 43, 44
Payton, Walter, 14, 19, 25, 32, 33, 40
Peete, Calvin, 18, 45
Pendleton, Terry, 45
Perry, Fletcher Joe, 41
Perry, Joe, 48
Perry, William, 39
Poage, George C., 8, 23, 30, 43, 45
Pollard, Fritz, 21, 26, 34
Puckett, Kirby, 45
Pullins, Al "Runt," 42

Reddick, Eldon, 18
Reed, Willis, 20, 46, 53
Ribbs, Willy T., 29
Richmond, Bill, 30
Rickey, Branch, 54
Robertson, Oscar, 7, 8, 43, 47
Robeson, Paul, 26, 27
Robinson, Frank, 11, 22, 37, 41, 52, 54
Robinson, Jackie, 7, 8, 10, 11, 13, 14,
   16, 22, 23, 24, 26, 37, 41, 42, 54
Robinson, Sugar Ray, 16, 24, 36, 43,
   44, 48
Rudolph, Wilma, 16, 24, 35, 36
Russell, Bill, 7, 23, 32, 42, 46, 47, 49, 52
Russell, Cazzie, 46
Ruth, Babe, 54

Sayers, Gale, 8, 19, 32, 48
Shelton, Bryan, 12
Schmeling, Max, 19
Scott, Wendell, 33
Shell, Art, 21, 34
Shippen, John, 44
Sifford, Charles, 12, 17, 18, 50
Simms, Billy, 43, 50
Simpson, O. J., 8, 13, 14, 19, 27, 33,
   35, 40, 48

63

Singletary, Mike, 27, 39, 48
Slater, Duke, 26
Smith, Emmitt, 32, 43
Smith, Ozzie, 46
Smith, Tommie, 14, 17
Smith, Walker, Jr., 15, 43
Spinks, Leon, 7, 31, 44
Spinks, Michael, 7, 31, 44
Stargell, Willie, 13, 36, 54
Stone, Lyle, 17
Strode, Woody, 28

Tatum, "Goose," 42
Taylor, Charlie, 28, 49
Taylor, Major, 50
Taylor, Otis, 51
Thomas, Debi, 17, 35
Thomas, Thurman, 43
Thompson, John, 32, 37, 41
Thurmond, Nate, 46
Tunnell, Emlen, 28, 41
Tyson, Mike, 8, 31, 33, 53

Unseld, Wes, 21
Upshaw, Eugene, 21

Young Anthony, 24
Young. Buddy, 48

Walker, Herschel, 32, 43
Walker, Melvin, 23
Washington, Kenny, 28, 34
Washington, Mali Vai, 44
Weathers, Carl, 39
West, Jerry, 37
Wharton, Jim, 29
White. Bill, 10, 14
White. Cheryl, 35
White. Dwight, 28
Wilkens, Lenny, 7, 21
Wilkes, Jamaal, 49
Willard, Jess, 29
Williams, Carl "The Truth," 53
Williams, Charlie, 53
Williams, Doug, 11, 22
Williams, Len, 53
Wills, Maury, 12, 19, 36, 37
Wiltshire, Charles, 33
Winfield, Dave, 20, 47, 52
Winfield, Paul, 45, 46
Winkfield, Jimmy, 53
Woodard, Lynette, 17
Worthy, James, 49

R. S. RENNERT has edited the nearly 100 volumes in Chelsea House's award-winning BLACK AMERICANS OF ACHIEVEMENT series, which tells the stories of black men and women who have helped shape the course of modern history, and the 10 volumes in the PROFILES OF GREAT BLACK AMERICANS series. He is also the author of several sports biographies, including *Henry Aaron, Jesse Owens,* and *Jackie Robinson.*